IT'S TIME TO EAT TATER TOTS

It's Time to Eat
TATER TOTS

Walter the Educator

Silent King Books
A WhichHead Entertainment Imprint

Copyright © 2024 by Walter the Educator

All rights reserved. No part of this book may be reproduced in any manner whatsoever without written per- mission except in the case of brief quotations embodied in critical articles and reviews.

First Printing, 2024

Disclaimer

This book is a literary work; the story is not about specific persons, locations, situations, and/or circumstances unless mentioned in a historical context. Any resemblance to real persons, locations, situations, and/or circumstances is coincidental. This book is for entertainment and informational purposes only. The author and publisher offer this information without warranties expressed or implied. No matter the grounds, neither the author nor the publisher will be accountable for any losses, injuries, or other damages caused by the reader's use of this book. The use of this book acknowledges an understanding and acceptance of this disclaimer.

It's Time to Eat TATER TOTS is a collectible early learning book by Walter the Educator suitable for all ages belonging to Walter the Educator's Time to Eat Book Series. Collect more books at WaltertheEducator.com

USE THE EXTRA SPACE TO TAKE NOTES AND DOCUMENT YOUR MEMORIES

TATER TOTS

It's time to eat, the clock says so,

It's Time to Eat

Tater Tots

The tummy rumbles, starts to grow.

A golden treat, so crisp and hot,

We're ready now for tater tots!

On the plate, they sit in rows,

A crunchy smell that tickles my nose.

With every bite, so warm, so neat,

Tater tots are such a treat!

Dip them in ketchup, swirl them around,

The happiest snack I've ever found!

Or maybe some cheese, gooey and bright,

Every tot is pure delight.

They're little and round, so easy to share,

Pass them around, show how you care.

Family and friends all gather near,

With tater tots, there's joy and cheer!

It's Time to Eat

Tater Tots

Crunch goes the sound, a perfect bite,

Every tot feels just so right.

Lunch or dinner, or snack in between,

Tater tots fit in any scene!

They come in a basket, or maybe a bowl,

A small tasty bite that fills the soul.

Potatoes cooked with love and care,

Tater tots are beyond compare!

Some like them plain, some like them spiced,

No matter the way, they're always nice.

With salt on top, or pepper for zest,

Tater tots are simply the best!

So grab your fork or use your hand,

It's tater tot time, isn't it grand?

No need to rush, no need to race,

It's Time to Eat

Tater Tots

Just enjoy each tot at your own pace.

When the plate is empty, the fun doesn't stop,

There's always more at the tater tot shop!

So remember this snack, so warm, so neat,

Hooray for tots, it's time to eat!

Now wipe your hands and give a cheer,

For tater tots, the food we hold dear.

Big or small, they're always just right,

It's Time to Eat

Tater Tots

A perfect snack, day or night!

ABOUT THE CREATOR

Walter the Educator is one of the
pseudonyms for Walter Anderson.
Formally educated in Chemistry,
Business, and Education, he is an
educator, an author, a diverse
entrepreneur, and he is the son
of a disabled war veteran.
"Walter the Educator" shares his
time between educating and creating.
He holds interests and owns several
creative projects that entertain,
enlighten, enhance, and educate,
hoping to inspire and motivate you.
Follow, find new works, and stay
up to date with Walter the Educator™